How to Paint Interiors

D1737060

WALLABY

A WALLABY BOOK
Published by Simon & Schuster
New York

Published by WALLABY BOOKS
A Simon & Schuster Division of
GULF & WESTERN CORPORATION
Simon & Schuster Building
1230 Avenue of the Americas
New York, New York 10020

WALLABY and colophon are trademarks
of Simon & Schuster

First Wallaby Books Printing May, 1981

10   9   8   7   6   5   4   3   2   1

Manufactured in the United States of America

Library of Congress Catalogue Card Number: 80-26467

ISBN: 0-671-42311-8

The advice in this book is based on careful research
and analysis. Due care should be taken in any repair
or maintenance program. The author and publisher
cannot take any responsibility for damage or injuries
caused by repairs or maintenance performed by
the reader.

Production: Jeffrey Weiss Group, Inc./Color Book Design, Inc.
Series Editor: Edward P. Stevenson
Design: Deborah Bracken, Design Director
Design Consultant: Robert Luzzi
Managing Editor: Barbara Frontera
Copy Chief: Donna Florence
Illustrated by: Jim Silks and Randall Lieu
Special Thanks to Jack Artenstein, Eugene Brissie, Jenny Doctorow and
Channa Taub

Table of Contents

Introduction

Painting is the quickest and least expensive way to bring new life and color to your home. With a rainbow of colors to choose from there's no end to the effects you can achieve.

There are paints on the market for practically any purpose you can think of. Some are best for use over plaster or wood, others for metal or brick, yet others specially made to resist moisture or prevent rust. Walls, windows, radiators, pipes— you can beautify and protect every surface in your house from attic to basement.

While painting is relatively easy, it's still a job you'll want to last as long as possible. There are three key factors to a professional looking job: choosing the right materials, surface preparation, and last but definitely not least, the right painting techniques. A little time spent in planning before you start can help you avoid mistakes that could prove expensive and time-consuming to correct.

This book tells you how to plan your painting job from start to finish. It describes the principal types of paint available on the market and the characteristics and advantages of each. It takes you through the world of colors and the magic they can work for you. It tells you which tools and materials to have on hand. And it gives you a practical, step-by-step approach to surface preparation and the painting itself—so that when you're finished you can sit back and experience that very special satisfaction that comes from a job well done.

Color

Before we get down to the nitty-gritty of hands-on work, let's consider the question of color—both how it affects us and some guidelines for picking a color scheme.

Color and Mind

In general, cool colors create a calm, tranquil atmosphere. Warm colors generate a greater feeling of activity, brightness, energy. Several kinds of practical considerations flow from this. For example, a room with a southern exposure that gets a lot of sun is a good candidate for a cool paint color to partially offset the warm effect of the sunlight. Kitchens, on the other hand, are rooms in which a lot of work and a lot of socializing take place. People tend to paint them in warm, bright, *up* colors that generate a feeling of energy.

Further, color affects our perception of space. Light colors are "recessive" and make a room appear larger. Dark or bright colors are "aggressive" and make a room appear smaller. So, if you want your ceiling to appear higher, for example, you could paint it white. If, on the other hand, you feel it is remote, "bring it down" by painting it in a darker shade—perhaps the same color as the walls. Walls can be made to "recede" or "advance" in the same way.

Finally, lighter colors demand less attention. They allow the eye to focus more on things *in* the room. Darker colors are more dramatic; they command more attention and become more of a focal point in themselves.

Choosing a Color Scheme

So much for the psychology of color. You are still left with the problem of picking colors, and with literally thousands to choose from, that task may appear formidable.

The first thing to remember is that color is *subjective*—a matter of taste. There are no hard and fast rules; no rights or wrongs. The best color is the one that *you* like the best. There is a lot of snobbery and mystique floating around about paint colors, but *you* are the person who must be pleased, not some decorator.

Fortunately or unfortunately, we are seldom in the position of picking a color scheme from scratch. There are many kinds of furnishings and other considerations that are likely to influence your choice of paint colors—the colors present in furniture, rugs, drapes, paintings or other artwork; colors in wallpapers, if one or more walls are to be papered; size, location, exposure and use of the room; and, finally, the color schemes of adjoining rooms. You will want your new paint to harmonize and reconcile as many of these elements as possible.

Simple or Complex

One of your decisions will be how many colors to use. Color schemes can vary from the utmost simplicity—white everything—to quite complicated arrangements where different walls are painted different colors, the ceiling in yet another color, and trim, moldings, etc., highlighted in bright colors of their own.

There are no rules, but this much is certain: the simpler you keep your color scheme, the fewer problems you will have making it work well. The closest thing there *is* to a rule is the principle that in any multi-colored scheme, *one color should always predominate*. Equal areas of different colors will always compete for attention.

Preparing Surfaces

One of the key "secrets" to a fine looking paint job is a well-prepared surface. The paint will never look much better than the surface it is applied to (another instance of a chain being no stronger than its weakest link). In some cases, if walls are in bad shape to begin with, proper preparation may be very time consuming. But it's *worth* it. So let's get down to business.

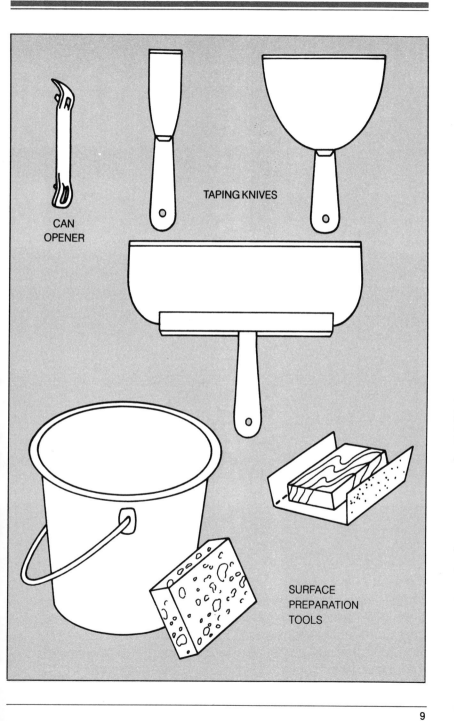

CAN
OPENER

TAPING KNIVES

SURFACE
PREPARATION
TOOLS

Clearing the Decks

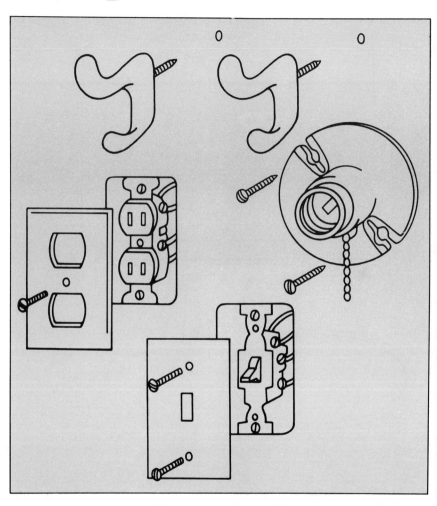

The first steps is to remove all that is removable from the room surfaces—light switch and receptical (electrical outlet) coverplates,
light fixtures, curtain hardware, door hardware and the like. Any of
these items that can't be removed should be carefully masked and
wrapped up for protection using masking tape and plastic film.

Patch and Plaster

The next stage is repairing the various wounds and scars in the wall surfaces. Here are some specific techniques for repairing cracks and holes in walls and ceilings of plaster and wallboard.

For Lath and Plaster Walls

Hairline cracks should be widened before filling so that the patching material gets a better hold. The best tool for this job is

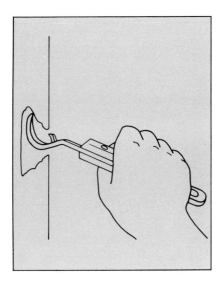

an old-fashioned can opener. The pointed end is sharp and

has a slight "hook" on it that enables you to undercut the edges slightly, which helps to hold the patching material even better. Once you have widened the crack, remove all loose material —blowing into the crack *with your eyes shut tightly* is a good way—and fill the crack using a

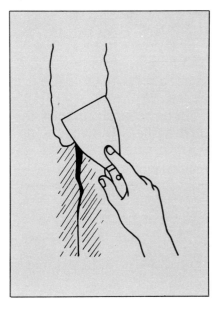

putty knife and spackle. (Spackle comes in two forms: a prepared vinyl compound used straight from the can, and a powdered kind that you mix yourself.) When the spackle is dry, usually the next day, sand it flat with a piece of medium-grade sandpaper wrapped around a small block of wood for flatness.

Small holes such as nail holes and miscellaneous small gouges that accumulate on walls are also easily repaired with spackle. Simply remove all loose material and fill the hole using the putty knife and spackle as above. Unfortunately, spackle shrinks somewhat as it dries, so it may require two or three layers of spackle (with drying time in between, of course) to get the repair flush with the surrounding wall surfaces. Sand the final coat, as above.

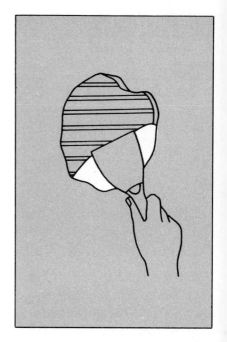

Large holes and cracks require a different approach. The specific materials and techniques will depend on the particulars of the case at hand.

Where the lath is more or less intact, it will be necessary to build up several layers of new patching material over that lath support. (The material marketed as "patching plaster"—as opposed to plaster of Paris or spackle—is best for this sort of job.)

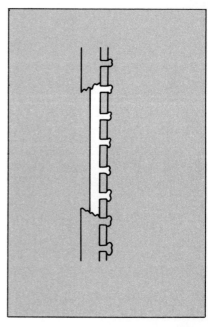

• Undercut the edges of the crack or hole as shown in the illustration.

• Clean out all loose material and then dampen the exposed plaster edges with water.

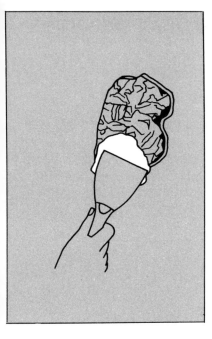

• Mix a small amount of patching plaster and apply a base coat to the wounded wall, working from the edges toward the center. Don't try to make the patch flush with the wall surface on this first coat.

• Let the first layer dry thoroughly (follow manufacturer's instructions), then dampen the surface and apply another layer. Depending on the depth and width of the hole, the process may have to be repeated two or three times, or until the patch is at least level with the surrounding surface.

• When the final layer is dry, sand it smooth and flat as for any repair.

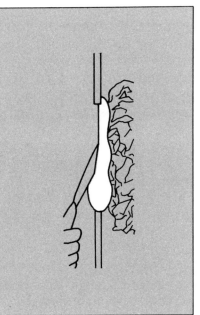

In cases where the lath is broken or absent, it will be necessary to provide some substitute surface to support the patching material. One simple method is to stuff the opening with wadded newspaper or coarse steel wool and apply the first coat of patching plaster over the stuffing. Additional layers of filler are added as necessary.

Another method utilizes a piece of wire screen as a substitute lath:

• Cut a piece of screen somewhat larger than the hole and loop a length of string through it approximately in the center.

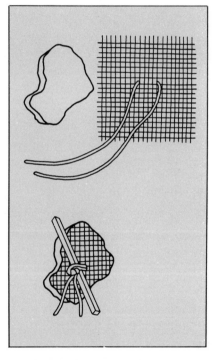

• Insert the screen into the hole, holding onto the string so as not to lose the screen inside the wall.

• Tie the ends of the string around a stick long enough to span the hole. A few turns of the stick to give a slight tourniquet-like tightening of the string should hold the entire assembly in place neatly.

• Apply a first layer of patching plaster, as above. When it is dry, cut the string off flush and continue adding additional layers of plaster as needed.

With either of these methods, of course, the finished repair is sanded smooth and flat.

For Wallboard

Repairs in gypsum wallboard are easily accomplished with the use of "joint tape," a strong paper tape about three inches wide, and "joint compound," a plaster-like material developed especially for use in joining the seams between wallboard panels.

Patch a crack, large or small, as follows:

• *Tear* off a length of joint tape about two inches longer than the crack on both ends. (Tearing, as opposed to cutting, gives a nicely "feathered" edge that doesn't leave a hard, straight ridge when you cover it with joint compound.)

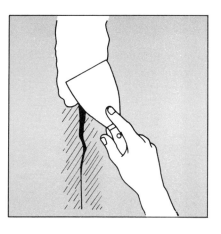

• Using a four-inch putty knife, known as a "taping knife," spread a band of joint compound along the crack area wide enough to accomodate the tape and long enough to extend beyond the tape ends.

• Lay the tape over the band of joint compound and press it firmly into place by running the taping knife over it.

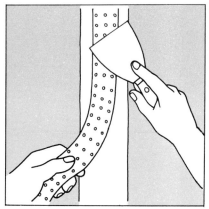

• Put another layer of joint compound *over* the tape, extending it an inch or so past the tape edges on either side and smoothing or "feathering" the edges down carefully.

• When the first coat is dry (about 24 hours), sand lightly, and then apply a third coat of compound that extends an inch or so past the previous one on all sides. Sand smooth when dry.

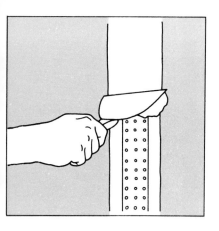

Note: The final smoothing or "feathering" may be done with a damp sponge rather than sandpaper. This method is handy and much neater, since it does not make a lot of dust, but don't overdo it. You can wash away all the joint compound if you aren't careful.

To patch a large hole in wallboard, you must cut a patch out of a scrap of wallboard to replace the missing material.

Besides the scrap, you will need special wallboard clips (available from the same sources as the board itself), a small "keyhole" saw, joint tape and joint compound. The repair is made as follows:

• Using the small saw, cut a patch somewhat larger then the hole, preferably in a rectangular shape, for the sake of simplicity.

• Place the patch over the hole and trace its outline in pencil on the wall around the hole.

• Cut out along the penciled outline so that the patch will fit snugly.

• Using the special clips, slip the patch into place in the hole.

• Cover the joint between the patch and the surrounding wall with joint tape and joint compound. Following the basic procedure outlined for patching cracks in wallboard. Tear the ends of the pieces of tape to approximate mitered angles. Finish as for all wallboard repairs.

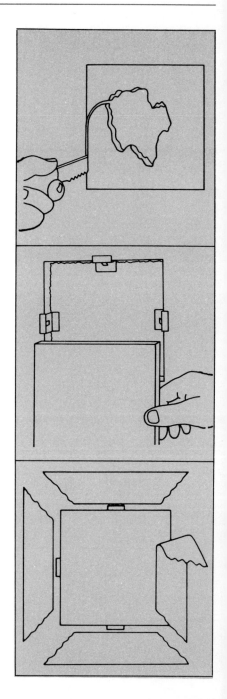

POPPED NAILS

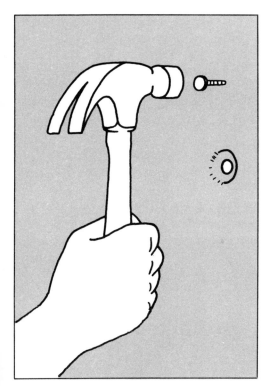 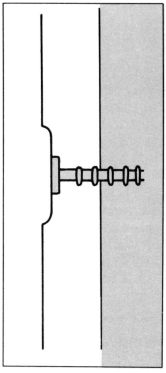

The nails that hold wallboard panels against the wall studs often loosen during the normal course of wear and tear, "popping" out from the wall surface. Take care of this problem by first hammering the nail gently but firmly back into its original position. The face of the hammer should drive the head of the nail between 1/32- and 1/16-inch below the surface of the wallboard and leave a gentle depression around the nail head which will later be filled with joint compound. Next, to secure the wallboard more firmly, drive a special "threaded" or "annular ringed" wallboard nail into the stud about three inches above or below the popped nail, setting it carefully just below the surface as before. Fill the indentations with joint compound, using a putty knife or taping knife. It will probably take two or three coats to get a perfectly flush, smooth finish. Sandpaper or sponge the final coat if necessary.

Old Wallpaper

If the walls you plan to paint are papered, you may face another task: You *may* have to remove the paper. If you're pretty sure that there is only one layer of paper on the walls and it is *firmly* attached, you may choose to leave it on the wall and paint over it without undue concern. If there are several layers of paper, and/ or if the paper is loose, peeling, "blistered," or flaking, it will have to come off.

Removal

Some wallpapers are "strippable"—that is, made to be easily removable. Just pry up a corner and peel each strip carefully off the wall.

Removing old non-strippable wallpaper involves wetting it so as to soften the paste that holds it on the wall, and then scraping it off with a broad-bladed knife or a special wallpaper scraper. Waterproof wallcoverings, such as vinyl, will have to be scratched or otherwise perforated so that the moisture can penetrate

(the teeth of a handsaw are good for this step.) There are two ways to speed and simplify the task of wallpaper stripping.

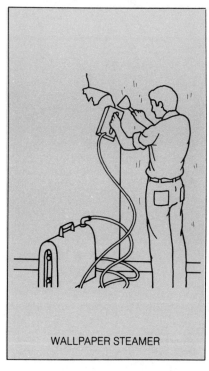

WALLPAPER STEAMER

The wallpaper "steamer" is a small portable boiler that pipes steam up through a tube to a "plate" that you hold in one hand while you work. The steam penetrates the paper quickly and makes the job go rapidly. Wallpaper steamers can be rented from many paint and wallpaper dealers who will supply you with full instructions for their use.

Chemical wallpaper removers are essentially "wetting agents" that help the water work its way through the fibers of the covering, softening the paste more quickly than water alone. Chemical removers are available from the same sources as steamers and also come with full instructions.

Old Paint

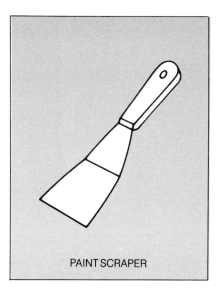

PAINT SCRAPER

As we mentioned earlier, your paint job will look no better than the surface it covers. if you are planning to paint over a previously painted surface, check to see if the old paint layer is still intact.

Scraping

Walls and (especially) ceilings often peel and flake. This is a result, generally, of too much paint on the surfaces, paint applied over dirty or greasy surfaces, incompatible layers of paint, or moisture getting into the wall or ceiling. Whatever the reason, all loose paint must be removed before you apply any new paint. This requires a paint scraper— the familiar broad-bladed knife,

not the "hook" scraper designed to smooth wooden surfaces. A paint scraper with a beveled or "chisel" edge will help you get under the layers of loose paint, but it also increases the risk of your gouging the plaster underneath. It's your choice, but be careful and be thorough. Get it *all* off.

Stripping

Woodwork is even more likely to have faulty paint than walls. This is because paint doesn't adhere quite as successfully to wood as it does to plaster, and because the heavier paint bodies usually used to cover woodwork build up more rapidly so there is generally a much thicker paint

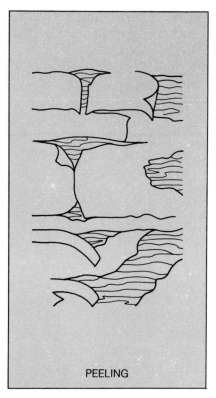

PEELING

BLISTERING

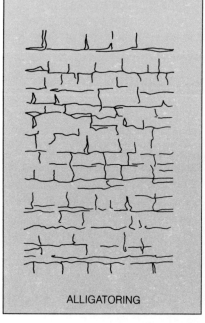

ALLIGATORING

layer. In case of severe chipping, peeling, "blistering," crazing, "alligatoring" or general deterioration, you will have to remove the old paint if you want a clean, new-looking surface for your new paint. Sometimes there is such a heavy accumulation of old paint on woodwork that you may want to strip it just to restore the crisp contours of the millwork (the moldings, etc.). Whatever the reason, if you decide to strip, you have a choice of methods: heat or chemical paint removers.

HEAT STRIPPING

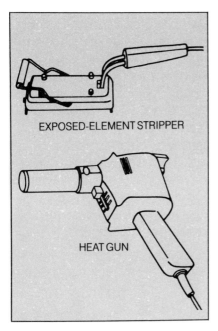

EXPOSED-ELEMENT STRIPPER

HEAT GUN

Heat will soften the old paint so that it can be scraped off the woodwork. The three available heat sources for this job are (1) the propane torch—the most dangerous, and *not* recommended; (2) the "exposed element" electric paint stripper; and (3) the "heat gun"—like a glorified hair dryer that blows super-heated air onto the surface. The heat gun is the safest, most efficient and, initially, the most expensive method. If you have a lot of woodwork to strip over a period of time, you may consider the investment worthwhile. With either of the first two devices, you must exercise great care not to get the work so hot that you scorch (or set fire to) the woodwork. Mastering the technique means finding the point at which the paint is soft enough to be scraped off easily without danger of burning the wood underneath.

CHEMICAL PAINT REMOVERS

Chemical paint removers are simpler to work with, in some ways, but they, too, are hazardous. The mixtures are all quite caustic and will cause skin irritations where they come into contact with your hands. Paint remover in the eye is an extremely painful and dangerous situation. Wear glasses or safety goggles to protect your eyes and rubber gloves to protect your skin.

There are many paint removers on the market, but most can be divided into two groups; liquids and "semi-paste" types. The liquids tend to be cheaper. Some work well, others not so well. The semi-paste types are almost all more expensive than liquids; as with the liquids, some are better than others. The two advantages of the paste types are: (1) They stay put on vertical surfaces, and (2) they don't dry out nearly as fast. The importance of the first is fairly obvious. The second is important because it takes *time* for a chemical remover to eat through all the layers of paint. Liquid mixtures tend to dry out before they have penetrated all the paint layers.

With paint removers, as with most things, you usually pay for what you get. A little more money spent up front may save a lot of your valuable time. Further, if you add up the expense of doing a large amount of paint stripping with chemical removers, both in terms of time and dollars, you may find that the investment in a tool like a heat gun is not so far out of line.

FINAL CLEANUP

Once you have removed the bulk of the paint from the woodwork, by whichever method you selected, you will be left with a residue of paint. An application (or an *additional* application) of paint remover will remove most of this, and the remainder will usually be cleaned up neatly with liberal application of a mixture of alcohol (shellac solvent) and lacquer thinner. A good supply of rags is necessary for this stage of operations.

Prime and Seal

Any new wall surface—and that includes patched and repaired sections as well as new plaster or wallboard walls—needs to be primed before any other finishing operation is carried out. The purpose of priming is to limit the absorbency of the wall surface and keep other finishes *on* the surface, not *in* it. Walls should be washed down before priming with a strong household cleanser or a solution of trisodium phosphate. Allow the walls or repaired areas to dry overnight before applying primers.

Plaster and Wallboard

Plaster walls and plaster and spackle repairs on plaster walls may be primed with either alkyd or latex primers. Wallboard walls, and any repairs where new wallboard is exposed should be primed with latex ("PVA") primer; as alkyd will raise the surface grain on the paper covering of the wallboard, and should not be used.

Note: Primers are not terribly different from the finish paints we use nowadays. One of the principal differences is, since they don't contain expensive pigments, they are *cheaper*. In a pinch, or where you have only a small area to prime, and the investment in a gallon of primer isn't justified, a preliminary coat of the finish paint will work fine.

Wood

New wood, like new walls, should be given a sealer coat before the final finish is applied. But before that, all exposed knots and sap streaks should be given a coat or two of shellac so that the resins do not "bleed" through the paint and cause a stain. (Shellac dries very rapidly, so this operation should not slow you down significantly.) Newly stripped wood should also get a sealer coat. Special primer-sealers for wood are available, but a slightly thinned coat of any alkyd paint will do just as well.

Metal

Metal—radiators, pipes, grilles and what have you—need to be primed with preparations that protect them and make them compatible with the chemical properties of the finish paints applied. Virtually all metal primers are patent formulas. Your paint dealer will be able to advise you on your needs. However, you must know *never to paint iron or steel with a water-thinned paint,* either as a primer or a finish coat. It will cause rust.

Painting Tools

In painting, as in any kind of work, having the right tools on hand can make all the difference between a frustrating, unpleasant experience and a rewarding, well-done job.

Clearly, the most important part of your painting equipment arsenal is the tools with which you actually apply the paint. Brushes, rollers and, more recently, painting pads, are all commonly used. While you may be able to do your whole job with just one of these kinds of painting tools, the most efficient job will result from the use of a combination of them. Brushes, for example, can paint any surface—and do a fine job—but rollers cover large areas three or four times faster, producing, if used properly, an excellent appearance. And, while special rollers and pads are being designed daily to take care of specific, difficult little areas, most of this kind of work can be done better with a brush.

How Good is Good Enough?

There are two predominant philosophies on painting tools. One suggests that tools be cheap and disposable. This saves greatly on the effort expended on cleanup. If you have a relatively small job to do and don't plan on doing a lot of painting over the long haul, this is a reasonable approach.

The other point of view says "buy the best tools you can afford—and take care of them." The idea here is that they will last for years and end up costing less in the long run.

There is much to be said for this philosophy from the economic point of view, if you can afford to shell out the cash up front. (If you consider how much money you are saving by doing the job yourself, it may not seem like such a large expenditure.) But there is an added bonus: GOOD TOOLS WORK BETTER than cheap ones, often *much* better. They are designed the way they are for good reasons and can make a job easier and more pleasant and produce a better result in the end.

Rollers

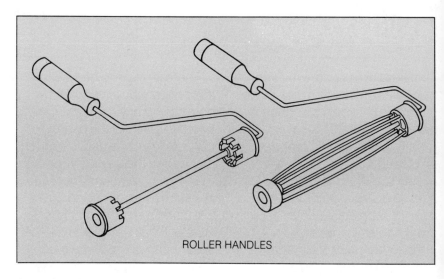

ROLLER HANDLES

Actually, the difference between the top of the line and the bottom, as far as rollers are concerned, is not so very great. Still, if you are interested in good results, it may be better to stay away from the bargain counter.

Rollers, of course, are two-part items: the roller handle and the cover. Roller handles, if they are sturdy and reasonably well made, differ little from one another in practical terms. The standard sizes are made to accommodate covers of 7- or 9-inch lengths. All but the cheapest have a threaded indentation in the bottom of the handle into which an extension pole can be fitted .

Covers come in several types, the main variation being the length and the texture of the nap or pile. (Although roller covers come with identifying names like "lambswool" and "mohair," virtually all are really made from synthetic fibers—mostly nylon or polyester.) Covers with smooth, short naps (⅛- to ¼-inch) are designed to produce a smooth finish on a smooth surface, usually with a semi-gloss or high-gloss paint. Covers with medium-length nap (⅜- to ½-inch) are designed for general-purpose painting. They tend to leave a slightly stippled surface

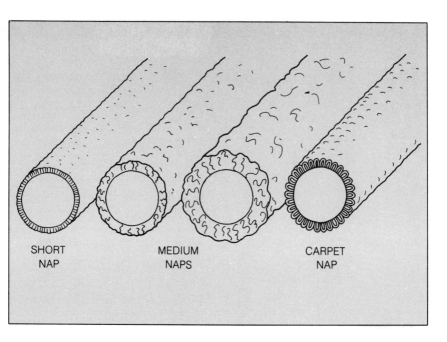

SHORT NAP   MEDIUM NAPS   CARPET NAP

which is appropriate to flat wall paints. Covers with very long naps (up to 1 inch, sometimes longer) are designed for applying paint to rough or irregular surfaces, such as brick, masonry, shingle, etc.

In addition, there are roller covers with special rough surfaces, such as tufted carpet or spongelike fibers, designed to create a strongly textured paint surface. These are special tools.

Roller covers vary considerably in quality, and that quality is reflected both in how well they do their job (stand up to paint) and how long they last. First, the cover must have a reasonably rigid tube, or the parts of the cover that are not supported by the roller handle assembly will not bear against the wall. Second, the nap or pile must be firmly and durably attached to the tube. Cheap roller covers self-destruct in an amazingly short time. With proper care in clean-up, a good roller cover can last for many jobs and many years.

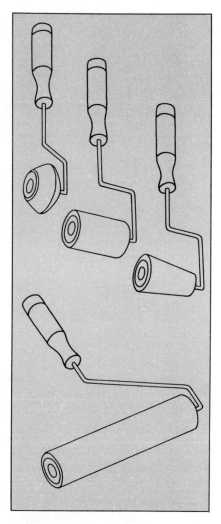

Brushes

It is safe to say that brushes are the most versatile class of painting tools, but there are brushes and there are brushes. Enough different types (as well as sizes, etc.) exist that it is well worth the time needed to become acquainted with them.

First, there are two broad categories of brushes—defined by the composition of their bristles. **Natural bristle brushes** (the finest ones made from hog bristle and/or ox hair) have been around for centuries. Two reasons prompted the development of **synthetic bristle brushes.** First, natural bristles can become waterlogged; the water in latex paints makes them flabby and ineffective. Second, natural bristles of high quality have become more and more expensive over the years while nylon (the synthetic material used for virtually all brushmaking) has become cheaper and better adapted to the task.

So, nylon brushes are a must for working with any water-thinned paint. Natural bristle brushes simply won't do a good job with these materials.

Nylon bristle brushes will also do a perfectly satisfactory job

As mentioned, rollers for general large-surface work come in standard 7- and 9-inch lengths. Smaller rollers (2½- to 3-inch) rollers are made for small areas. Small doughnut-shaped and conical rollers are made for painting corners and for edging.

with alkyd and other non-water-thinned paints, but for these, a good natural bristle brush will do a *better* one. Natural bristle brushes are unquestionably more expensive for tools of roughly equal quality—probably 50% higher, but there is a point on the quality ladder past which nylon bristle brushes do not climb. The choice, then, depends on your personal feeling about the tools you work with and the quality of the results you expect.

What Do We Mean By Good?

What characteristics make one brush better than another? From one way of looking at the question, the answer is simple—the brush that gives the best-looking job with the least effort. To do a good job, a brush must (1) hold paint well. (It is the means of transferring the paint from container to wall); (2) spread that paint efficiently and with a minimum of effort (bristles must be both resilient and organized); and (3) not leave bristles on the paint surface.

What does this all mean? Let's pick up a good brush. Its bristles are gently curved—in toward the tip. They are tapered—

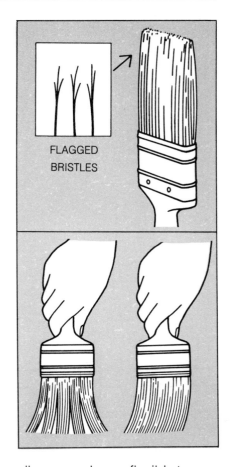

FLAGGED
BRISTLES

slimmer and more flexible toward the tip. The bristles are "flagged" at the ends—that is, they have lots of what we might just as well call split ends, which hold the paint. Press the bristles against the palm of your hand. They don't splay out in a random messy pattern, rather they remain in a coherent configuration, bending together and retaining a coherent shape. This is

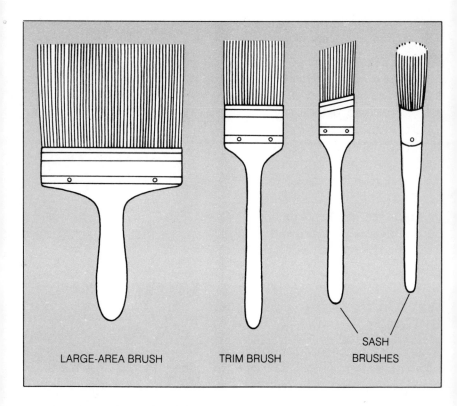

LARGE-AREA BRUSH   TRIM BRUSH   SASH BRUSHES

very important for maintaining control of *where* you are spreading paint. Finally, examine the brush for loose bristles. There are bound to be a few in any new brush. Remove any you find, then rap the handle sharply on the table or counter. Spin the brush between your palms. If the brush is well made, further shedding will be minimal.

Brushes from 4 to 6 inches wide, usually with the "beavertail" type of handle, are for painting large areas. Brushes of 2- to 2½-inch width are generally used for trim and small-area painting. Some of these have longer handles which give the painter greater control. Small brushes, 1 to 1½ inches wide, are used for touchup, for small, hard-to-reach areas, and for painting window sash. Special sash-painting brushes come in two styles. Some painters prefer one, some the other. The more common is a flat brush with the bristles cut at an angle. The other type is round or oval.

Pads

Pads for large-area painting are generally rectangular—approximately 4 by 8 inches. Smaller pads in various shapes and sizes are designed for specific tasks such as sash painting. One special pad applicator has small nylon rollers built into one edge so you can paint clean, neat edges at ceiling lines. Another padlike painting tool is the disposable foam "brush." These come in a variety of sizes from about 1 to 2½ inches in width. New patent painting tools appear on the market all the time. If these intrigue you, your paint dealer will be able to show you a selection of the latest offerings.

What Do I Really Need?

The basic painting kit, to do the job efficiently, should contain: one 7- or 9-inch roller with cover(s) appropriate to the paint and surfaces you will be dealing with; one or two 1½- to 2½-inch trim brushes; one sash-painting brush.

For roller painting you will need:

• A roller pan or tray. It acts both as a paint reservoir and a means of loading the roller evenly. Some sort of similar tray is necessary if you are going to use pads.

• An extension pole or poles. Useful, if not absolutely essential, extensions come in a variety of lengths and thread into the end of the roller handle, enabling you to paint high walls and ceilings without a ladder.

General painting accessories that you will need include:

• *Drop cloths* to cover and protect your floors and furniture. Fabric drop cloths are more expensive than the plastic kind, but work better. If you plan to do a lot of painting, they might be a worthwhile investment.

• *Masking tape,* to mask edges, windowpanes, hardware, etc.

• *A stepladder* will be helpful for painting ceilings, high woodwork, etc.

• A medium sized *bucket* or *pail* to carry paint to the work area when you are using a brush.

• *Painting guides* to help you paint areas adjacent to floors and other unpainted surfaces and to paint straight lines.

• *Mixing paddles* to stir paint are made in wood and plastic and are often available for free when you buy your paint. A special mixing device called an "impeller" which attaches to an electric drill helps to take the drudgery out of mixing paint.

• An abundant supply of clean, absorbent *rags* or *paper towels* for cleaning up the inevitable drips and spills.

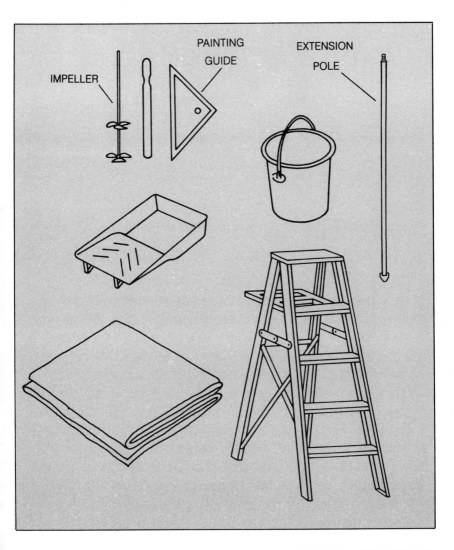

Choosing Paint

E very paint is composed of three essential elements—
the *pigment,* the substance that imparts color; the *base*
or *binder,* which form the film, when the paint is dry, that
"binds" the pigment to the painted surface; and the *vehicle,*
the medium that thins the mixture and makes it liquid.

There is an astonishing number of different paint products
on the market these days, each competing for your attention
and dollars. The array is bewildering, but it should simplify
your task to realize that, with the exception of a few specialty
items, virtually all of these products fall into two basic groups:
alkyd-base paints and **latex-base** paints. Alkyd and latex
paints each have specific properties that determine their
suitability for a particular job.

Alkyd Paints The Durable Ones

Paints with bases of synthetic resins called alkyds must be thinned with chemical solvents such as mineral spirits or other "paint thinners," and cleanup requires the same kinds of solvents.

Alkyd paints make an extremely tough and durable film, which makes them highly resistant to moisture and grease and makes them easy to clean. They generally *adhere* much better than latex paints, and, for that reason, they can be successfully applied over a greater variety of surfaces.

They have a few disadvantages, however, mostly derived from the chemical nature of the vehicle: they dry relatively slowly, they do have an odor, requiring adequate ventilation both during work and while they are drying; and finally, they are more expensive and difficult to clean up after. These disadvantages are at least balanced by their excellent lasting properties and the richness of their look, making them the paints of choice for high-traffic areas and for any job where only the best will do.

Alkyd paints are often referred to as *"oil-base"* paints, a term left over from the days in which most housepaints were made with a binder of natural resins— usually tung oil or linseed oil. Those natural resin bases have been gradually replaced by synthetic ones, like alkyds, to the point where nowadays true oil-base paints are a real rarity. The term persists, however, and can be taken to mean "alkyd."

Latex Paints The Easy Ones

The resins used in latex paints— mostly polyvinyls and acrylics— are soluble in water, so water is the vehicle used for thinning and cleanup. That fact contributes to the following advantages of latex paints: with no chemical solvents, they are almost odor-free, and they are cheaper and easier to clean up after. Another big advantage is that they dry very quickly—usually within an hour or two. This means that it is rarely a problem to give a wall or a room two or more coats in the same day.

The other side of the coin is that latex paints are less durable, less washable and less resistant to moisture or grease than alkyds, and, some painters feel, they do not give quite the depth or richness of appearance. Nevertheless, they are *so* easy and convenient to use that they are by far the most popular paints on the market.

While we tend to associate the word "latex" with natural rubber, the actual meaning of the word in this case is simply "a milky liquid." Latex paints contain no rubber of any kind.

A Choice of Finishes

Interior paints come in any of three "finishes," or degrees of sheen: flat, semi-gloss and high-gloss. Latex paints are available in flat and semi-gloss; alkyd paints in all three finishes. The higher the gloss, the more durable the paint film is, and the easier it is to wash.

Flat finishes (without gloss) give a soft, elegant look. They are traditionally used for walls and ceilings in living rooms, dining rooms and bedrooms. One of the advantages that flat-finish paints offer is their ability to *de*-emphasize imperfections in the surface underneath.

Semi-gloss finishes (also known by trade names such as "eggshell," "lustre," and the like) are quite versatile. They are often used to paint woodwork and trim in rooms with flat-painted walls. They also make an excellent, durable and easily washable wall finish. Ceilings are seldom painted with semi-gloss.

High-gloss finishes, the shiniest of the three, are traditionally used for trim and woodwork, especially in kitchens, bathrooms, children's rooms or wherever a bright, clean look and easy washability are desired. As the attempts to manufacture truly high-gloss latex paints have not yet been entirely satisfactory, you will need to turn to alkyd-base paints if you wish to get a true high-gloss effect.

Enamels

In the days of true oil-base

paints, some mixtures included some natural varnish resins to impart an extra sheen to the paint film. These paints were called enamels. Today, the term has ceased to have that specific meaning—varnish added—but it has persisted in the trade and means exactly the same thing as high-gloss paint.

Special Finishes

There is an increasing number of specialty items on paint dealer's shelves these days. They include special products for coating surfaces such as acoustical tile, brick, cedar shingles, and the like; all manner of stains, varnishes and other transparent finishes for wood; paints with special chemical and physical properties, such as epoxy resin paints, waterproof rubber-based paints, etc.; and finally (and of most concern to the average home painter) the primers and sealers used to prepare various kinds of new surfaces for their finish coats of paint. Of this last category, latex primer (also called PVA or polyvinyl-acrylic primer), alkyd primer, shellac and various trade brands of metal primers are most likely to be called for in the typical home painting situation. Their uses

and applications will be discussed later on.

Custom Mixed Colors

Time was when your selection of paint colors was limited to the number of factory-blended colors that your dealer could afford or had the space to stock on his shelves. The development of store-mixed "custom" colors has expanded the home painter's palette of color choices dramatically. Paint manufacturers are now able to supply dealers with a selection of tints and a machine that precisely measures and dispenses them so that formulas for literally thousands of subtle shades can be duplicated easily and reliably. Working from instructions supplied by the manufacturer, the dealer actually mixes the tints for you on the spot.

While it is wonderful to have such a wide range of colors to choose from, there are a few slightly negative factors to take note of:

• Custom colors are more expensive than comparable stock colors, often substantially so.

• While custom mixing is accurate, it is not as accurate as factory blending in large batches. As a result, there may be slight color differences from can to can or between the actual paint and the color sample card.

• Virtually no dealer will take back custom colors for a refund, so if you plan to use a custom shade, figure your quantity needs carefully.

Choosing the Right Paint

To get the best possible results from your labor, you must be sure to use only materials that are *compatible* with each other and with the surfaces you apply them to. In questions of product compatibility, your paint dealer is your best source of information. Consult him or her whenever you have the slightest doubts or uncertainty.

As far as surfaces are concerned, there are several classic mismatches:

• Latex paint over iron or steel will produce rust. Metal surfaces require priming with a preparation formulated for that purpose followed by a finish coat of alkyd or other non-water-thinned paint.

• Alkyd paint or primer over new, unfinished wallboard will produce a "raised nap," or fuzzy surface. The proper coating for new wallboard is latex (PVA) primer, which can then be painted with the finish coat of your choice.

• Any paint, alkyd or latex, applied over knots or sap streaks in new, unfinished lumber is likely to lead to stains or "bleed-through." Knots and sap streaks should be primed with a coat of shellac, best followed by a coat of alkyd primer over the whole surface of the new wood.

• Latex paint, especially semi-gloss, applied over any high-gloss finish will produce the effect known as "alligatoring"—a crazing of the paint finish resembling alligator hide— unless the surface is roughened before painting either by rubbing with sandpaper or steel wool or by using one of the commercial preparations, such as Liquid Sandpaper, made especially for the purpose.

How Much Should I Buy

Estimating

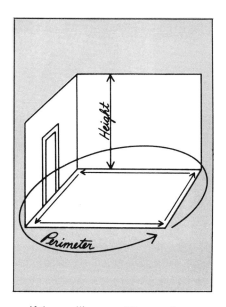

The area covered by a gallon of paint varies from product to product. A general rule of thumb is that one gallon of a base coat will cover 450 square feet of wall; one gallon of finish coat, about 500 square feet. It is a good idea to have a pretty clear estimate of the quantity of paint you will need before you head off to the paint store, but it is *essential* that you have an accurate estimate of the *area* to be painted.

To calculate the area of your room:

• Measure the perimeter of the room and the height of the walls. Round off your measurements *upward* to the next whole foot.

• Multiply the perimeter by the height. This gives you the area of the walls in square feet.

• To find the area of the ceiling, multiply its length by its width.

If the ceiling and the walls are to be painted the same color and finish, add the areas together. If not, keep the totals separate. You may get a rough estimate of the number of gallons of each type of paint required by dividing the area in question by 450 (the average coverage of a gallon of paint) and rounding *upward* to the next whole gallon.

Windows, doors and other trim are usually painted with different color and/or finish from the rest of the room. Note the number of windows and doors, and the amount of trim generally, and consult your paint dealer. Two quarts to a gallon of paint will usually cover the woodwork and trim.

Painting Techniques

I t may strike you as unnecessarily complicated, but painting is really a three-stage process. The stages are: (1) getting the paint *on*to the surface, (2) spreading the paint, and (3) smoothing the surface. Understanding this breakdown can speed work and make for a better result.

Brushwork

Laying On

The first step in painting is called "laying on." The aim is to transfer as much paint from the container to the wall in one step as you can, *without spilling paint*. Efficiency is the objective here.

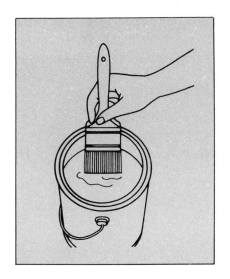 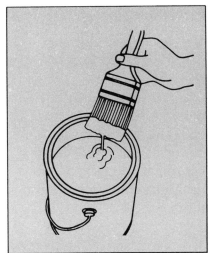

1. Dip *no more than ⅓ of the length of the bristles into the paint.*

2. Gently wipe excess paint off on the rim of the container.

3. Quickly transfer the brush to the wall and make a broad zigzag stroke in the area you wish to cover.

Spreading

The second stage of brush painting is called "cross-brushing." First, you must decide in which direction the final brushstrokes will run. For walls and vertical trim, this will usually be vertical; for horizontal trim, horizontal. For ceilings, it will usually be across the width of the room.

1. Begin spreading the paint by brushing in parallel strokes *in the direction of the final strokes*.

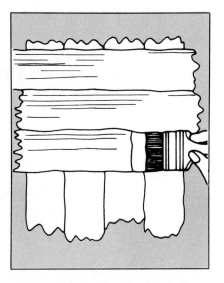

2. Once the paint is spread fairly well, brush *across* (at a 90° angle to) the first brushstrokes. This both helps to spread the paint more evenly and to work the paint into the surface, eliminating small skips or "holidays."

Smoothing

The final stage of brush painting is called smoothing or "feathering."

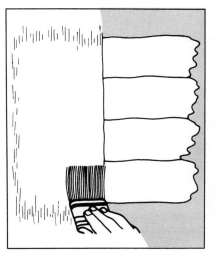

1. Brush over the cross-brushing in the direction of the final brushstrokes as determined previously. Make these strokes even and parallel.

2. Go over the area one final time using just the very tips of the bristles and lifting the brush carefully at the end of each stroke. This should produce a smooth, even paint surface.

Rollerwork

Loading

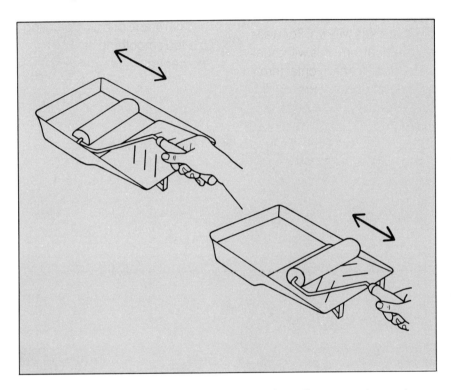

Dip the roller into the paint tray. (The paint should not be more than about ½-inch deep in the reservoir.) Cover the whole roller cover, *if you can;* some paints are so thick that it is quite difficult to roll the roller once you have paint on one side of it.

Use the spreading area of the tray to distribute the paint evenly over the roller cover. It may be necessary to go back to the reservoir for more paint, once you have partially distributed it. As with a brush, the objective here is to get as much paint onto the wall as possible in one operation *without spilling,* so use the spreading part of the tray to squeeze out the excess.

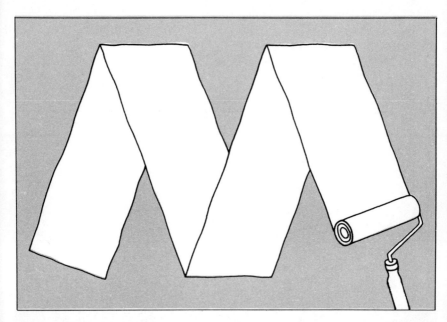

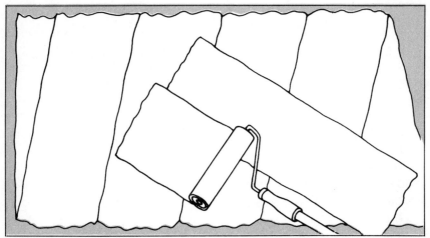

Laying On

With the roller properly loaded, transfer it to the area you wish to paint and make a broad zigzag.

Roll over the initial zigzag with parallel strokes of the roller, going in the direction that you plan to finish in. Then cross those strokes at a 90° angle.

Finishing

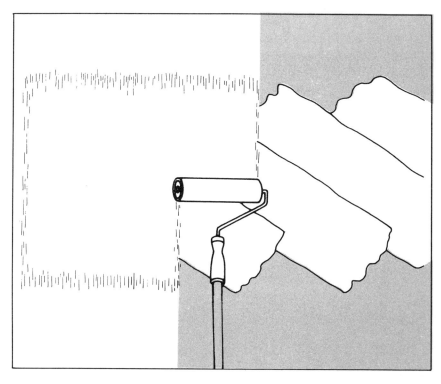

Finally, using an unloaded roller, carefully roll over the area again in the direction you have chosen for the finish strokes, overlapping strokes, and being careful to obliterate the ridges that mark the ends of the rollers when there is too much paint on the surface. Be careful also in applying and removing the roller at the beginning and ends of your strokes. (The direction of rollerstrokes is somewhat less critical than brushstrokes since the slightly stippled effect produced by most general roller painting hides the strokes fairly effectively. It is the ridges that tend to give the game away.)

Roller painting tends to produce a lot of fine spatter—tiny specks of paint that get all over everything. This can be kept to a minimum, if it constitutes a problem in your painting situation, by rolling *slowly*. This may slow the pace of the work somewhat, but it can save you cleanup time.

General Considerations

Whatever method you are using, work in one limited area at a time. The area that seems to be convenient for roller painting is about one square yard. For brush or pad painting, the area should be about half that—about 4 to 5 square feet. Finish each area, then start a new area adjacent to it, blending from each new area into adjacent already-painted ones. Part of the feathering or smoothing operation is making blends between new and already painted sections.

Pads

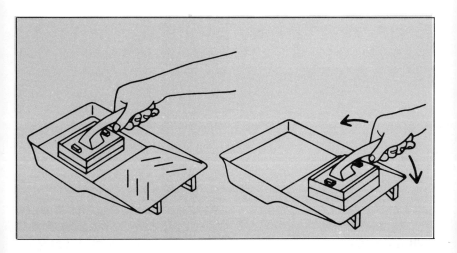

Painting with pad applicators is somewhat like a cross between brush and roller painting, but the general idea is the same.

Loading

Load the pad by immersing the fibers in the paint reservoir. (Be careful not to get paint on the holder; it will drip.) Wipe off excess paint on the edge of the tray so that paint will not drip.

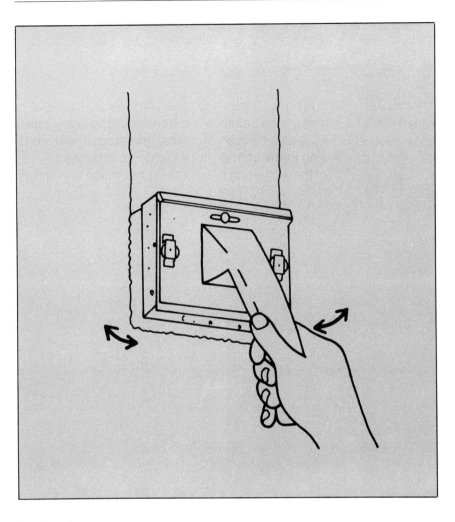

Laying On

Transfer the applicator to a section of the wall. Make bold strokes with the pad to distribute the paint quickly.

Spreading and Finishing

With overlapping strokes, spread the paint evenly; cross the first stroke directions; finally, finish up with careful, parallel feathering strokes.

Special Brush Techniques

Cutting In

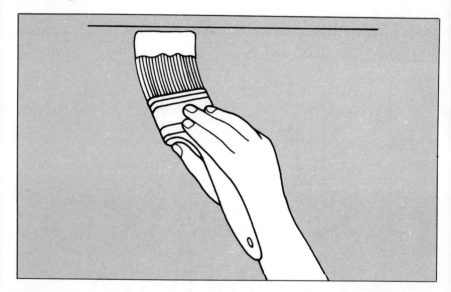

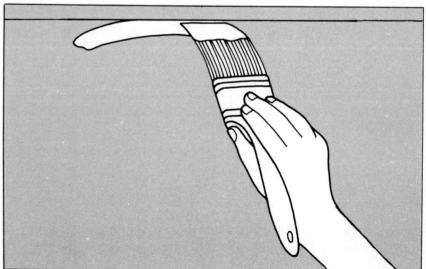

Cutting in (sometimes called "beading") is a technique for painting clean, straight edges at places where one color of paint begins and another leaves off, such as the top edge of a colored wall meeting a white ceiling. One color, usually the lighter one, is lapped over the corner and the second color "cut in" to the corner line. The technique makes use of the structure of the brush to keep the line straight.

First, load the brush a bit more sparingly than usual. Next, bring the loaded brush up to the line you wish to work to. Start your stroke a bit below the ceiling line, keeping the width of the brush parallel to that line. The bristles should hold together and form an accurate straight edge which you will find you can control easily. Paint slowly and reload your brush frequently. Cutting in is a fairly painstaking technique, but you will get faster and better at it. You can achieve the same effect using masking tape, but it is costly and time-consuming to mask and there is always the danger of pulling off the fresh paint when you remove it.

Painting Window Sash

Painting window sash ("sash" is both singular and plural) is probably the slowest, hardest of all interior painting operations. To make it as easy and painless as possible, use the right tools, i.e. brushes (or pads) specifically designed for the task.

Besides the frame, the window channels, the parting strip, etc., each window has *at least* four wood-to-glass strips to paint; windows with muntins (the strips that separate the panes) have many more. Painting muntins is just a question of doing lots of careful cutting in. One of the problems is getting into the many inside corners involved. This is where the angular brush has advantages over other types: the point is particularly suited to getting those pesky parts covered. The other thing that makes it easier is understanding that some paint *should* get on the glass for a proper seal. A bit of trimming and scraping with a razor knife after the paint is dry will clean things up very neatly. Some painters religiously mask each pane of glass, but this takes twice as long as proper painting and subsequent trimming, and, if you don't get the tape off the glass fairly promptly, it becomes *very* difficult to remove.

Final Preparations

ow that you have chosen your color scheme, prepared your walls and other surfaces, bought your paint, got your painting tools together, and learned how to use them, you are all ready to begin. Right? Wrong! Believe it or not, there are still a few final preparations to take care of.

Dress for battle in old clothes and shoes that you don't mind getting paint on. Cover yourself up as much as possible without restricting your movements or making yourself uncomfortable. A hat is recommended, even if you are not painting ceilings. Painter's caps are sometimes supplied free by dealers. Otherwise, use a ski cap, a bandana or grandpa's old fedora. Gloves will help with later cleanup, especially if you're using alkyd paint. Inexpensive plastic painting gloves provide the best protection, although they are not very comfortable to wear.

Final preparation of the work area involves removal of as much of the contents as possible and making sure all remaining surfaces that are not to be painted are somehow protected

After all this is done, it is time it WASH the room—all the surfaces you are going to paint. It is necessary to clean these surfaces of all dust, dirt and grease if the paint is to adhere properly, so do a *thorough* job

While you are waiting for your walls to dry (or just before you are ready to paint), you should open your first can of paint (or primer). Eliminate the problem of paint accumulating on the lip of the can every time you pour by making a series of five or six holes in the rim, using a hammer and a common nail to pierce the metal. This will allow the excess paint in the lip to drain back down into the can.

Next, the paint must be mixed. Most paints (but *not all*) require mixing prior to use to insure that all the components are evenly distributed. Read the instructions on the label. If it says DO NOT MIX, then just use the paint as it comes from the can.

Most paints, however, *do* require mixing. If paint stocks sit on the shelves for long periods, the components separate. The dealer will generally "pre-mix" the paint you buy with a mechanical vibrator at the time of purchase, so if you just bought your paint, the chances are that it will not need extensive mixing. On the other hand, if you have had it around for a long time, or if the dealer neglected to mix it for you, the mixing will take a while —perhaps five to ten minutes. Using a paddle (or any flat stick) or an "impeller," mounted in your electric drill, mix the paint until it appears uniform and there is no longer any concentration of pigment at the bottom of the can.

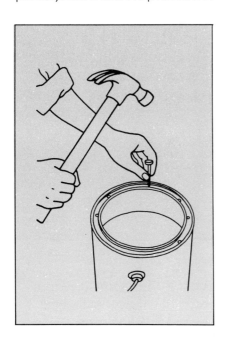

Where to Start

O ver the years, painters have developed a sequence of work that makes the job go more quickly, with less wasted effort, and gives a better-looking result. In general, you paint the large surfaces first, working from the top down. This means that you start with the ceiling, then paint the walls. Then you go on to the trim, the doors and the windows. (The order of the last is not critical.)

To reiterate, the order is:

1. Ceiling

2. Walls

3. Trim

4. Doors

5. Windows

When painting adjacent areas with different paints, either different colors or different glosses, make sure that the first paint is *dry* before painting the new, contrasting area.

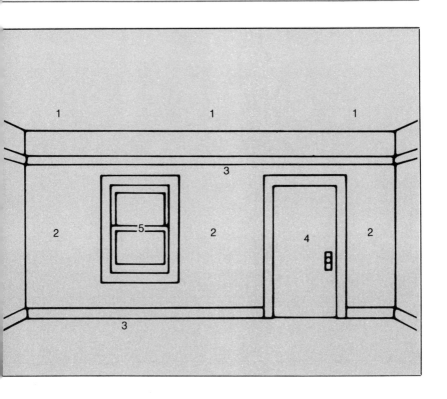

Painting Ceilings

Painting the ceiling needn't be difficult, especially if you use a roller and an extension pole of the appropriate length. It is important both for comfort and control that your extension be long enough so that you can work at a comfortable angle. If you have to hold the pole more or less vertically while working, you will tire quickly and have a difficult time controlling the direction of the roller.
The shallower the angle at which you work, the easier it will be.

Try to paint the whole ceiling at one stretch so you can avoid lap marks that inevitably result when wet paint is applied over dry. Follow these steps:

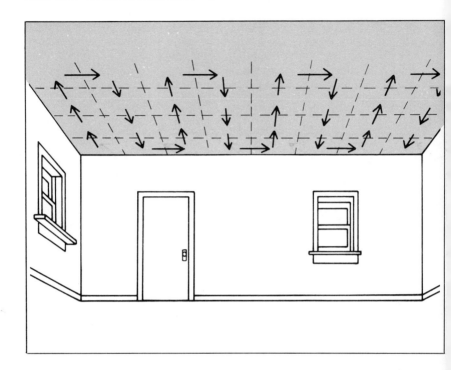

1. First, paint a 2- to 3-inch strip around the edge of the ceiling, using either a medium sized brush or an edging or corner roller. This strip is necessary because the large roller can't paint very close to the edges of walls or ceilings. If walls and ceilings are to be painted with the same paint, you may as well lap down the walls an equal amount (two to three inches). If the walls are to be a different color, you still need to lap over the wall-ceiling joint a bit—say an inch or so. When the walls are painted, you will "cut in" the top of the wall (see p.49).

2. Paint the main area of the ceiling with the roller, working in small sections. Blend newly painted sections into already painted sections (including the brush-painted areas).

3. Join sections into strips across the narrower dimension of the room (i.e., the width), completing one strip before going on to the next. Work systematically and the job will go *faster*.

Painting Walls

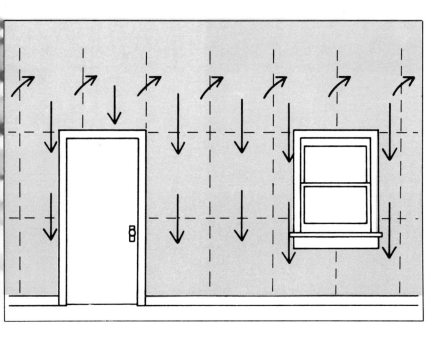

Like ceilings, walls should be painted entirely in one stretch to avoid lap marks.

1. First, paint a 2- to 3-inch strip around all the as-yet unpainted perimeter of the wall using a brush or edging roller. If the wall is being painted a different color from the ceiling, this is the point at which you will have to *carefully* cut in the wall color against the ceiling color at the top of the wall.

2. With the large roller, paint the main area of the wall, working in small sections that join up into either vertical *or* horizontal strips. (Some people prefer to work *across* the wall in order to avoid having to remove and reinstall the extension handle repeatedly.) Finish one section before going on to the next, blending newly painted sections with already painted sections as before.

Painting Trim

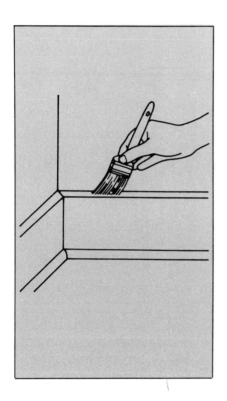 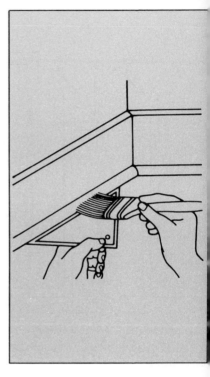

Moldings and baseboards will require a bit more care and concentration than painting walls and ceilings. There is a good deal of careful cutting in to be done.

If you have a picture molding on the wall near the ceiling, it can be used as a convenient dividing line between colors. It should be painted with a sash brush *after* the surrounding wall areas are painted.

Baseboards are perhaps more easily painted in a two-stage operation. Paint the top edge first, cutting in against the wall paint with a small sash brush. The lower portion of the baseboard can be painted with a larger brush and a painting guide used to protect the floor.

Painting Doors

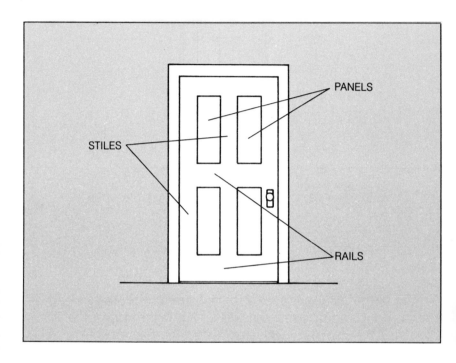

Doors, especially "paneled" doors have their own painting sequence. The parts of the door have names and it will be simpler to use them in discussing the work sequence. The recessed oblong areas are the **panels**, the horizontal members are the **rails**, and the vertical members are the **stiles**. The painting work proceeds in the following sequence:

• Paint the panels, starting with the molded edges, and finishing with the main areas. Work from side to side and from the top downward.

• Paint the rails, starting with the top rail and working down.

• Paint the stiles.

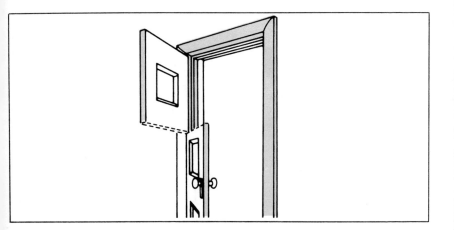

• Paint whichever vertical *edge* of the door is visible when the door is open.

• Paint the door frame, beginning at the top and working down the sides.

• Paint all the inside surfaces of the door frame that are exposed when the door is open. Use the inside surface of the **stop** as the dividing line if the color outside the room is different from inside.

• The surface of a plain door is painted much as if it were a wall—in small sections blended into one another as you join them into strips, working systematically. Plain doors can also be painted with rollers if you wish.

Painting Windows

Traditional double-hung window sash are constructed, like doors, of horizontal rails and vertical stiles, with the addition of **muntins**, the small strips that divide the panes. Use a sash brush to paint the rails, stiles and muntins; use a larger trim brush for the larger areas.

If you have decided to mask the edges of the glass with tape rather than to cut in carefully and scrape afterwards, do that now.

Before beginning to paint, raise the lower (inner) sash about ¾ of the way up, or as high as you can get it. Lower the upper (outer) sash as far as it will go. Now, begin to paint in the following sequence:

• Paint the inner sash in the following order: vertical muntins, horizontal muntins, rails, stiles. Do not paint the top of the upper rail.

• Paint the outer sash in the same order, as far as you can conveniently reach.

• Reverse the positions of the sash without fully closing the window. Finish painting the outer sash. Paint the top of the upper rail of the inner sash.

• Paint the surrounding frame and sill.

• Finally, paint the channels in which the sash run up and down: First lower both sash and paint the three pieces, the parting strip, the jamb, and the stop on the upper half of the frame. When these are dry, raise both sash and paint the lower part.

Note: Move the sash frequently during and after painting to prevent sticking.

Cleanup

The Work Area

Even if you have been careful to protect your floors and other not-to-be-painted surfaces, a quick check will almost certainly reveal numerous spots and drips that got by your dropcloths somehow. Clean them up before they have a chance to dry.

For **latex paints,** use soap or detergent and water and a clean cloth, sponge or paper towel to scrub off spots. For **alkyd paint,** use mineral spirits or other paint thinner and a clean rag or paper towel.

Your Tools

Among your painting tools and accessories there will be some inexpensive items such as paint mixing paddles, plastic drop cloths, paint guides, perhaps even inexpensive brushes, which are easier to throw out than clean.

Tools you wish to keep—this usually means good brushes, roller covers and/or paint pads—must be thoroughly cleaned. They will have to be "washed" out in enough changes of the appropriate solvent so that there is *no* paint residue left. Fortunately, for brushes and roller covers there is a delightfully easy alternative; the spinner or centrifuge.

But first, the "conventional" method. The procedure is pretty much the same for brushes, roller covers and pads.

- First, wipe off as much excess paint as possible on old newspapers or paper towels.
- Remove roller covers and pads from their handles, then proceed:

For latex paints

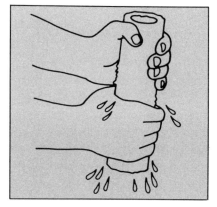

Fill your sink part way with warm water. Add a bit of liquid detergent. Work the tool in the soapy water until the paint has loosened. Change the water, add detergent and repeat the procedure—as often as necessary until the paint is entirely removed and the water remains clear. It may take six or eight changes to get a roller cover *really* clean; brushes and pads are somewhat easier.

For alkyd paints

Pour some solvent into a container large enough to accommodate your tool. Work the tool through the solvent until the paint becomes loosened. Change to fresh solvent and repeat.

At this stage, you have an option: either continue cleaning with changes of fresh, clean solvent, *or* switch to a concentrated household cleaner that "cuts fresh paint," such as Lestoil. Pour a small amount of the cleaner into the container and work the tool around in it briefly. Rinse with clean water. Repeat this procedure with the cleanser two or three times. The tool should now be quite clean. This alternative saves a great deal of (relatively) expensive solvent.

The Easy Alternative

The invention of the brush spinner or centrifuge marked a turning point in the lives of painters. It is now possible, with the use of this relatively inexpensive tool, to clean paint brushes and rollers in a fraction of the time that it used to take, *and* get them *cleaner* at the same time.

The principle is simple. Thin the paint residue with some of the appropriate solvent and then spin the tool at high speed. The paint is literally thrown off the fibers of the brush or roller by centrifugal force. Two, three, or at the most, four repititions of this simple procedure and the tool is perfectly clean and ready to be put away for storage. To go over it again, slowly, here's the procedure:

• Insert the brush or roller cover into or over the jaws of the spinner.

• Rinse the tool in the proper solvent; remove as much paint as possible.

• Spin the tool vigorously by pumping the handle up and down several times rapidly *with the spinner held inside some container*—an old wastebasket

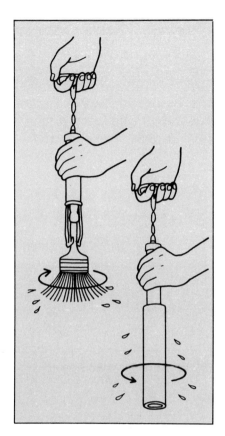

Odds and Ends

• Clean off your roller and pad handles with the proper solvents.

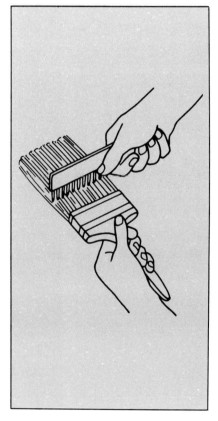

with a plastic liner, or even a brown grocery bag inside a plastic garbage bag, will do.

• Repeat this entire procedure —rinse, blot, spin—once or twice. The brush or roller cover should be quite clean.

• For maximum cleanliness, wash the tool once in household cleanser as outlined above. Spin it again and it will emerge squeaky clean and almost dry.

• Brushes should have their bristles combed straight. Use either a special brush comb or an old wide-toothed hair comb.

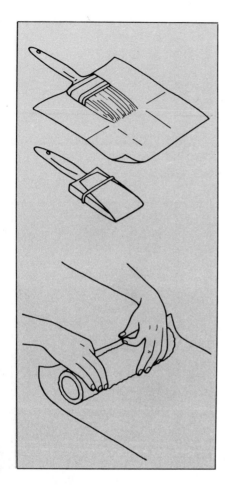

Even if you don't have much paint left, store it for future touch-ups:

• Using a paint stirrer, put a dab of paint across the lid to identify the color and mark the level of the leftover paint on each can.

• Wipe off the outside and rim of the paint cans with a paper towel.

• Press the lid into place and tap down all around with a hammer.

• Allow paint tools to dry, then wrap them in their original coverings, heavy brown paper or aluminum foil.

• Store brushes by hanging or laying on a flat surface. Rollers should be stored standing on edge so that the nap will not flatten. Store pads on a flat surface, pad side up.

• Store until needed. Oil-based paints and solvents are flammable and should be stored away from heat sources such as boilers and furnaces. A metal cabinet is an ideal storage space.